VOTE
VOTE
VOTE

GOVERNMENT IN AUSTRALIA
THE CITIZENS HAVE VOTED
John Lesley
REDBACK publishing

First Published 2026 by
Redback Publishing
Suite 6, 13a Narabang Way,
Belrose NSW 2085
Australia

www.redbackpublishing.com
orders@redbackpublishing.com

ISBN 978-1-761401-14-5

Author: John Lesley
Editor: Caroline Thomas
Designer: Redback Publishing

Original illustrations © Redback Publishing 2026
Originated by Redback Publishing

MIX
Paper from responsible sources
FSC™ C001507

A catalogue record for this book is available from the National Library of Australia

CONTENTS

What Is Voting? 4
Why Vote? 6
Australian Electoral Commission 8
Federal Electorates 12
Votes for Women! 14
Indigenous Australians 16
Citizenship and Voting 18
Becoming a Citizen 20
Rights of Citizens 22
Responsibilities of Citizens 24
Citizenship Ceremony 26
Not Yet 18? 28
Voting and the Constitution 30
Glossary 31
Index 32

WHAT IS VOTING?

When a group of people get together to make a decision, or to elect a person to do something important for them, they are engaging in casting a vote.

You might vote at school to elect a class captain.

You might vote around the dining table at home to decide where the whole family will go on holiday.

Voting for politicians

When we are referring to voting for politicians, a similar process applies. People who are eligible can vote at an election for the candidate they want to represent them in the government, whether that is for Australia, a State, a Territory or a local council.

I Vote

In Australia, all eligible citizens are expected to vote at government elections and referendums as a part of their civic duties.

Each voter only has one vote

Voting more than once at a single election is against the law and could lead to imprisonment.

Voting for the Senate

Some methods of voting at elections for governments do not involve selecting an individual candidate. A voter may select a political party. This happens in voting for the Australian Senate.

WHY VOTE?

One of the most basic rights and responsibilities of citizens in a democracy is voting.

Voting is the main way that citizens play a part in the law-making process, by electing representatives to Federal, State and Territory governments and to local councils. The men and women who win elections represent the people who live in their electorates (or wards in local council areas).

In the Federal, State and Territory Parliaments, elected members make and amend the laws that affect everyone, including non-citizens and those who voted for someone else who did not win enough votes to be elected. In local council elections, the councillors elected can make rules about where you can walk a dog, or how much noise you can make at a party.

Voting is a way to have a say in how you are governed. In some Australian elections, a very small number of votes have made a big difference in determining which candidate won.

Is voting compulsory?

In Australia, all citizens from the age of eighteen must enrol and have their name marked off the register in Federal, State, Territory and most local elections. Penalties apply if they do not do this without a valid reason. While it is not compulsory to fill in the ballot paper, it is compulsory to have your name marked off the electoral roll to show that you either attended the polling centre or cast a vote by mail.

In some democratic nations around the world, voting is not compulsory. Examples include the United Kingdom, the USA, Canada and New Zealand.

AUSTRALIAN ELECTORAL COMMISSION (AEC)

The Australian Electoral Commission, AEC, is an independent organisation responsible for conducting Federal elections, referendums and national plebiscites. It is not responsible for elections held by the governments of the States or Territories, or for local council elections. However, the same electoral roll of voters is used for all those elections.

Eligibility

Voting in Federal, State and most local elections is compulsory for all citizens once they turn eighteen years old. It is up to the individual to ensure they are officially enrolled to vote by applying to the Australian Electoral Commission. The electoral roll is a list of all the eligible voters who live in an electorate and who have applied to be enrolled. Penalties may apply if an eligible person fails to enrol and to have their name marked off the roll during an election.

People who are sixteen can apply to be enrolled so that they are listed and ready for when the next election occurs. Even if they are enrolled, they cannot actually cast a vote until they turn eighteen.

POLLING PLACES

A polling place is the name for the location where people can go to vote. Polling places are set up in schools and halls in every electorate.

When an Australian citizen goes to a polling place, someone from the Australian Electoral Commission marks the voter's name off a list of all the people on the electoral roll and the voter is given the ballot paper or papers.

The person voting makes their choice on the ballot paper and then slips it into a special ballot box.

SECRET BALLOTS

Elections for governments in Australia involve secret ballots. This stops electors being forced to vote for a candidate through fear of reprisals.

When a person votes, he or she stands in a private booth so no-one else can see what they are marking on their ballot paper. Secret ballot voting was first used in Australia in the 1850s.

COUNTING VOTES

At the end of voting, the ballot boxes are sealed and guarded with high security. The AEC counts all the votes and announces the results as soon as possible.

Scrutineers are people appointed by the AEC to observe the counting and ensure that every vote is counted correctly. This task is a very important part of the democratic process of government in Australia.

Voting in local council elections is not compulsory in some areas, so voters need to check what the rules are for where they live.

LOCAL COUNCIL ELECTIONS

Voting at Federal, State and Territory elections is only available for Australian citizens who are eighteen or older and are enrolled in their electorate. Each person is only allowed to vote once at any election.

Local council elections are a bit different. In some council elections, an Australian citizen who is a ratepayer but not a resident of the area may be allowed to vote. If they own property in multiple local government areas, they may be allowed to vote in each of them. Even a corporation may be permitted a vote, through the director or company secretary.

There are about 27 million people in Australia. Eighteen million of them are eligible to vote at elections. (AEC 2025)

FEDERAL ELECTORATES

A Federal electorate is the area represented by an elected Member of the House of Representatives. Australian Senators represent a State or Territory, not an electorate.

150
AUSTRALIAN ELECTORAL DIVISIONS

16
WA

2
NT

10
SA

Australia is divided into 150 electorates (in 2025), with about the same number of voters in each. This means that each Member of the Australian House of Representatives represents roughly the same number of people, which is just over 100,000. Some electorates are huge in area, while others are comparatively small.

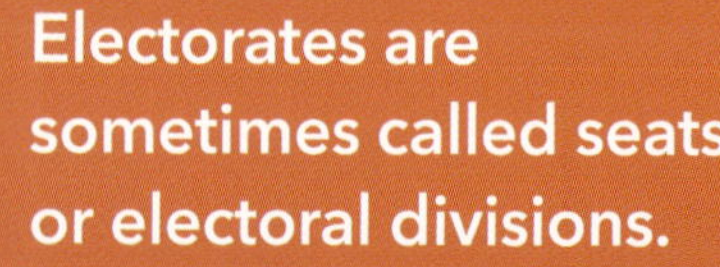

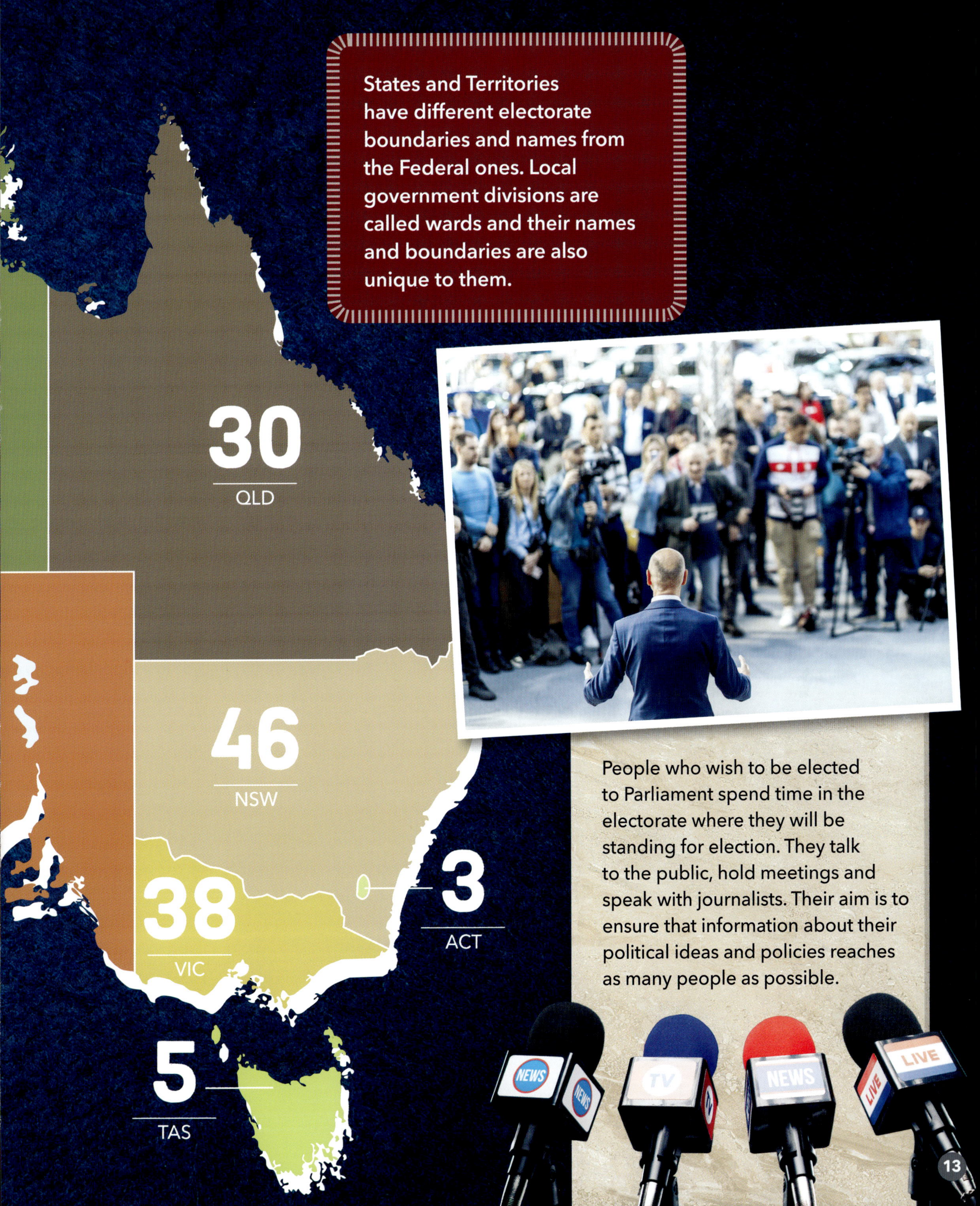

States and Territories have different electorate boundaries and names from the Federal ones. Local government divisions are called wards and their names and boundaries are also unique to them.

People who wish to be elected to Parliament spend time in the electorate where they will be standing for election. They talk to the public, hold meetings and speak with journalists. Their aim is to ensure that information about their political ideas and policies reaches as many people as possible.

VOTES FOR WOMEN!

THE RIGHT TO VOTE

The right to vote in government elections is called suffrage, and it is one of the most important rights a citizen has. The groups or types of people who have had this right have changed over time.

Australian men have had the right to vote in government elections since long before Federation, but women and Indigenous Australians used to be excluded.

In 1894, South Australian women were granted the right to vote, followed by Western Australia in 1899, New South Wales in 1902 and finally Victoria in 1908. Non-Aboriginal Australian women were granted the right to vote for the Commonwealth Parliament in 1902, and women voted in the 1903 Federal election. This was also the first time women were eligible to stand as candidates for Federal Parliament.

WINNING THE RIGHT TO VOTE

Many Australian women passionately believed in their right to vote. At the meetings and public rallies they organised, their catchcry was "Votes for Women", and they called themselves suffragettes.

In 1902, after much campaigning, women finally gained the right to vote in Federal elections. The women's campaign then moved on to wider issues such as women's rights as workers and mothers.

Despite gaining the right to vote in State and Federal elections, women were not allowed to actually stand for election to the State Parliaments until the end of the First World War.

VIDA GOLDSTEIN

The first woman to stand as a candidate in Australia and in the whole British Empire was Vida Goldstein, a leader in the women's suffrage movement. She ran an unsuccessful campaign for the Senate in 1903.

INDIGENOUS AUSTRALIANS

The 1967 Referendum

In 1967, the Australian people voted in a referendum to change parts of the Constitution concerning Indigenous Australians. More than 90% of voters said 'Yes' to the proposed changes. This gave the Federal Parliament the right to make laws for Indigenous Australians, and to include them in any national census.

Contrary to popular belief, this referendum did not grant any voting rights.

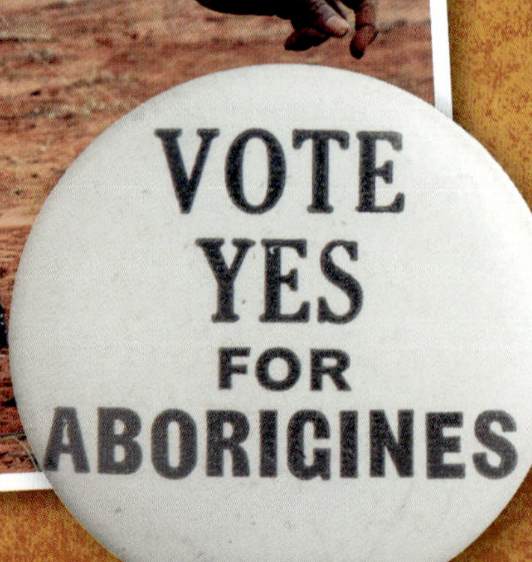

VOTING TIMELINE

In the original six Australian Colonies, voting rights for Indigenous Australians varied. After Federation, they continued to be excluded from voting for many years.

1902 - Australian men and women, except for Indigenous Australians, could vote in Federal elections

1949 - Indigenous Australians who had served in the armed forces could vote in Federal elections

1962 - Non-compulsory voting at Federal elections was introduced for all Indigenous Australians

1967 - Indigenous Australians had to be included in the census

1984 - Voting became compulsory for Indigenous Australians

CITIZENSHIP AND VOTING

Only Australian citizens can be listed on the electoral roll and cast a vote

So what is a citizen?

An Australian citizen is an official member of the Australian nation. Australian citizens are people who were born in Australia or who have been granted citizenship by the Australian Government. Being an Australian citizen means having many rights that are protected by law, but also certain responsibilities, such as a responsibility to vote at each election.

When did it begin?

Citizenship has only officially existed in Australia since 1949. Before then, there were no official Australian citizens. At that time, Australians were called British subjects. It was not until the Australian Nationality and Citizenship Act 1948 passed into law that Australia's British subjects became Australian citizens.

Unlike the original wording in the Australian Constitution, the Citizenship Act did not specifically discriminate against Indigenous Australian people. However, their rights as citizens were limited by laws passed by the States.

BECOMING A CITIZEN

There are several ways people may become Australian citizens

- A person born in Australia, and who has at least one parent who is an Australian citizen or permanent resident, becomes an Australian citizen at birth.
- An eligible person who migrates to Australia may be granted citizenship.
- A person might also obtain citizenship by descent. A parent who is an Australian citizen with a child born overseas may register their child as an Australian citizen.

Resident or Citizen?

People who come to live in Australia from overseas do not automatically become Australian citizens. Some people become permanent residents, while others hold a temporary residency visa. Temporary residents have some rights while in Australia, but not the full rights of citizens.

What is a Permanent Resident?

A permanent resident is a person who has been granted permission by the Government to live in Australia permanently. These residents have most of the same rights and responsibilities as Australian citizens. They have the same access to health care and education, but they cannot stand as a candidate in or vote in Federal, State or Territory elections.

RIGHTS OF CITIZENS

Some citizenship rights only belong to citizens over a certain age, such as the right to vote, but most rights are shared by all Australian citizens, regardless of age.

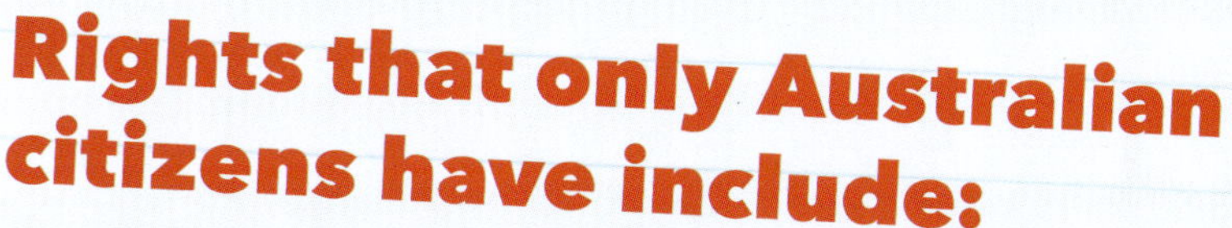

Rights that only Australian citizens have include:

- When over the age of eighteen, the right to vote in Federal, State and local government elections.
- The right to stand for election at Federal, State, Territory and local government levels.
- The right to have an Australian passport.
- The right to apply to join the Australian Defence Force.
- The right for a child born overseas to Australian parents to become an Australian citizen by descent.

RESPONSIBILITIES OF CITIZENS

Australian citizens have many freedoms, but they have responsibilities as well.

Australian citizens are required to accept the basic structures and principles of Australian society, such as:

- Equality of opportunity
- Freedom of speech
- Freedom of religion
- Equality between people
- Freedom to join legal groups and associations
- Having English as the national language

Australian citizens are also expected to:

- Obey laws made by Australia's governments.
- Enrol and vote at Federal, State, Territory and most local government elections.
- Serve on a jury, if requested.
- Defend Australia, if called upon, by serving in the Australian Defence Force.
- Not commit treason by assisting any enemy in armed conflict against Australia or the Australian Defence Force.

Discrimination

In Australia, citizens and others need to be aware that it can be illegal in a number of situations to discriminate against a person based on their sex, age, race, disability or gender orientation.

Responsibilities in Defence

In the past, Australian troops have fought in a number of wars. As an Australian citizen, a person has the responsibility to fight for Australia if ordered to by the Australian Government. This is called being drafted, or conscripted. Between 1965 and 1972, thousands of Australian men were conscripted to fight in the Vietnam War. Since then, no Australian citizen has been conscripted to fight in a war.

CITIZENSHIP CEREMONY

If a person meets the requirements, and wishes to become an Australian citizen, he or she must attend a citizenship ceremony. At the ceremony, the new citizen recites the Australian Citizenship Pledge. This is the final stage of becoming an Australian citizen. Citizenship ceremonies are happy events, and new citizens are welcomed as full members of Australian society.

The citizenship ceremony is usually held by the local council in the area where the applicant lives. The citizenship certificate received is a very important document and should be kept in a safe place.

AUSTRALIAN CITIZENSHIP PLEDGE

From this time forward, under God,
I pledge my loyalty to
Australia and its People,
whose democratic beliefs I share,
whose rights and liberties I respect, and
whose laws I will uphold and obey.

A person may choose to make the pledge with or without the words 'under God'.

NOT YET 18?

Young people who are interested in politics and the processes of government can still become involved, even if they are not yet old enough to vote.

Visit Parliament

Watch from the public gallery as the politicians debate and vote on bills.

SRC

Join a Student Representative Council and find out how a group of people with a social or political agenda operates.

More ways to get involved:

- Political parties often allow young people from the age of sixteen to join and attend meetings.
- Keep aware of issues arising in the community, and of how they are being reported by news services.
- Remember that politics is a hothouse of ideas, so don't be misled by the loudest voice or by information sources that you have not checked for accuracy.

VOTING AND THE CONSTITUTION

Sections 7 and 24 of the Australian Constitution of 1901 specify how the new government of the nation will be elected. It will be "directly chosen by the people of the Commonwealth" (for the House of Representatives) or "directly chosen by the people of the State" (for the Australian Senate). The Constitution does not specify who or what a citizen of Australia is. Since 1901, this has led to many debates in Parliament over the exact nature of Australian citizenship.

Voting has been compulsory in Federal elections since 1924, but this was not a requirement in the Constitution in 1901.

Women voting for the first time in Queensland, 1907

GLOSSARY

ballot .... process of voting

candidate .... person who is seeking election to government

catchcry .... slogan that is used to inspire a group

census .... official counting of the population

civic .... referring to matters dealing with citizens and government

compulsory .... required by law or some proclamation

conscription .... forced entry into membership of the armed services

electorate .... defined area in which a voter lives

eligible .... having met all requirements

politician .... person who is or who seeks to be elected to government

referendum .... vote held to change the Constitution

scrutineer .... person who checks the counting of votes

suffrage .... right to vote in elections

treason .... act by a citizen meant to harm their own nation

18+

INDEX

AEC 8
Australian Defence Force 22, 24, 25
Citizenship Pledge 27
conscription 25
democracy 6, 7, 10
electoral roll 7-9, 11, 18
electorate 6, 9-13, 31
Goldstein, Vida 15
House of Representatives 12
local councils 5-9, 11, 23, 24, 26
permanent resident 20
referendum 5, 8, 16, 31
seats 12, 13
secret ballot 10
Senate 5, 12, 15, 30
suffrage 14, 15, 31

Acknowledgements
Abbreviations: l–left, r–right, b–bottom, t–top, c–centre, m–middle
We would like to thank the following for permission to reproduce photographs (images © Shutterstock unless otherwise stated): Pg3br Nils Versemann / Shutterstock.com, pg6b ChameleonsEye / Shutterstock.com, pg7bl ChameleonsEye / Shutterstock.com, pg7br Nils Versemann / Shutterstock.com, pg8t Nils Versemann / Shutterstock.com, pg8m Nils Versemann / Shutterstock.com, pg8b Nils Versemann / Shutterstock.com, pg9b Nils Versemann / Shutterstock.com, pg14m spatuletail / Shutterstock.com, pg15t State Library of New South Wales, pg15m Museums Victoria, pg16tr ChameleonsEye / Shutterstock.com, pg16bl Di Vincenzo / Shutterstock.com, pg16br Museums VictoriaPhotographer: Jon Augier, CC BY 4.0 <https://creativecommons.org/licenses/by/4.0>, via Wikimedia Commons, pg19m Bennography / Shutterstock.com, pg21b Alex Cimbal / Shutterstock.com, pg22m Rose Marinelli / Shutterstock.com, pg22b Ryan Fletcher / Shutterstock.com, pg24br wisely / Shutterstock.com, pg25ml The Mariner 4291 / Shutterstock.com, pg25mr Ryan Fletcher / Shutterstock.com, pg 26m Bennography / Shutterstock.com, pg27b DIAC images, CC BY 2.0 <https://creativecommons.org/licenses/by/2.0>, via Wikimedia Commons, pg28ml Luckies / Shutterstock.com, pg32b Nils Versemann / Shutterstock.com, pg30b State Library of Queensland.

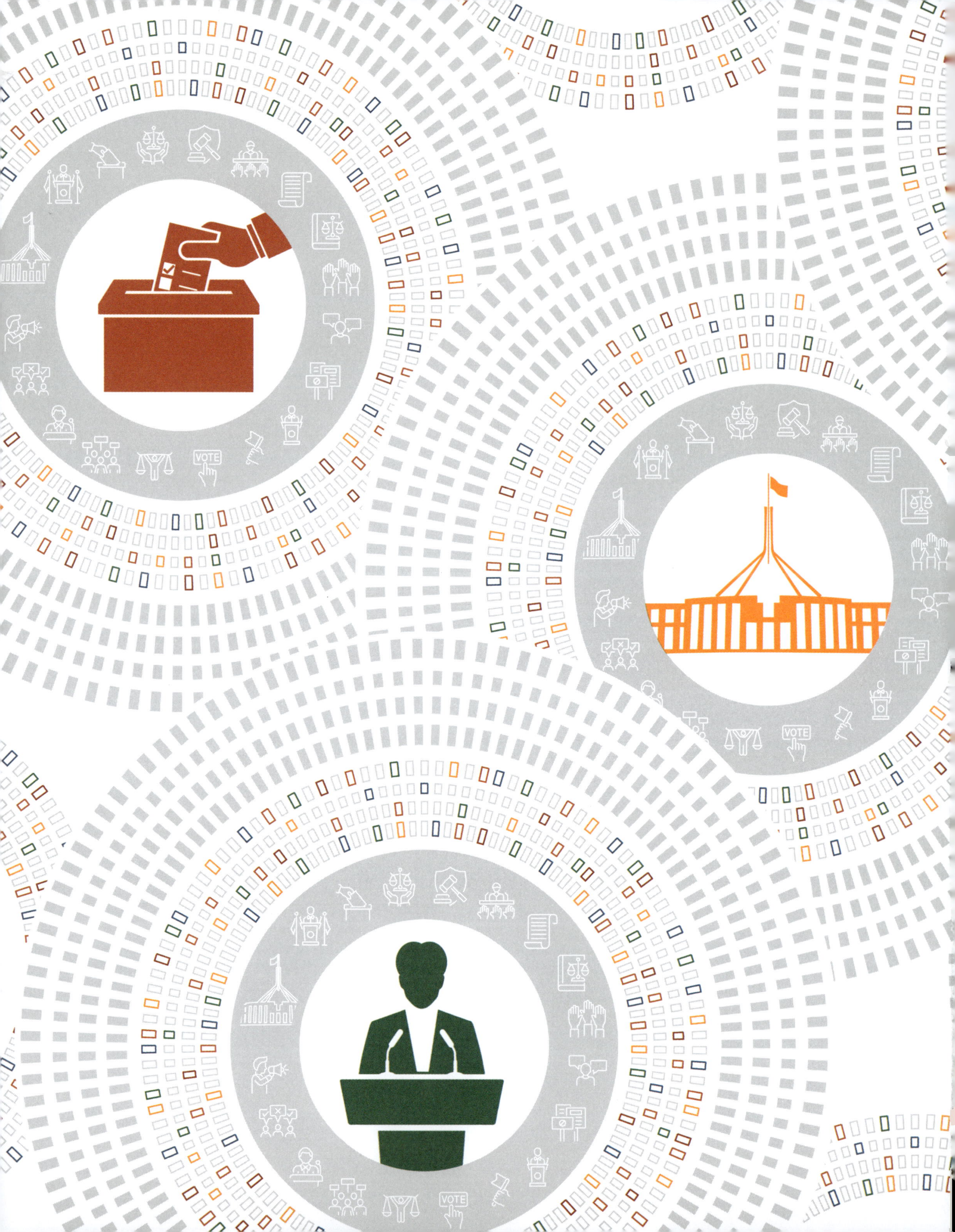
VOTE
VOTE
VOTE